Messy GOES TO OKIDO

Volcanic panic

Hello, I'm Messy. What's your name?

My name is

....

Thames & Hudson

Let's go to OKIDO!

Sing along to the OKIDO song with Messy.

Messy goes to OKIDO,
Find out what you want to know,
Let's all go to OKIDO,
OKIDO, OKIDO!

Messy goes to OKIDO,
All the things you want to know,
Come along let's say hello,
Let's go see our friends …

Come and
meet my friends.

Felix!

Zoe!

Felix!
Zoe!
Zim, Zam, Zoom!
Balabalaboomboom!

Messy goes to OKIDO,
Let's all go to OKIDO,
Find out what you need to know,
MESSY GOES TO OKIDO!

Find Foxy

Where is Foxy hiding
in the story?

A clue – look among
a group of animals.

Zim!

Zam!

Zoom!

One day, Messy, Felix and Zoe spotted a flock of birds flying past. One of the birds flew down to them. It seemed to be trying to tell them something.

Tweet!
Tweet!

Why aren't you going with your friends, little bird?

I think she wants us to follow her.

The gang **jumped** in Okidoodle and followed the bird all the way to the ocean. Messy switched his car to boat mode and they **splashed** into the water.

Follow that bird!

I wonder where she's taking us?

Splash!

The bird led them to a desert island. There was a towering mountain in the middle.

As they pulled up on the beach, they heard a loud grumbly, **rumbling** noise. Then the ground began to **shake!**

It's coming from the mountain!

Rumble!

Shake!

Hey, mountain. Are you okay?

The mountain apologized for all the noise.
She told them that her name was Vivian
and she was actually a volcano. She said her
insides were feeling all **rumbly** and bubbly.

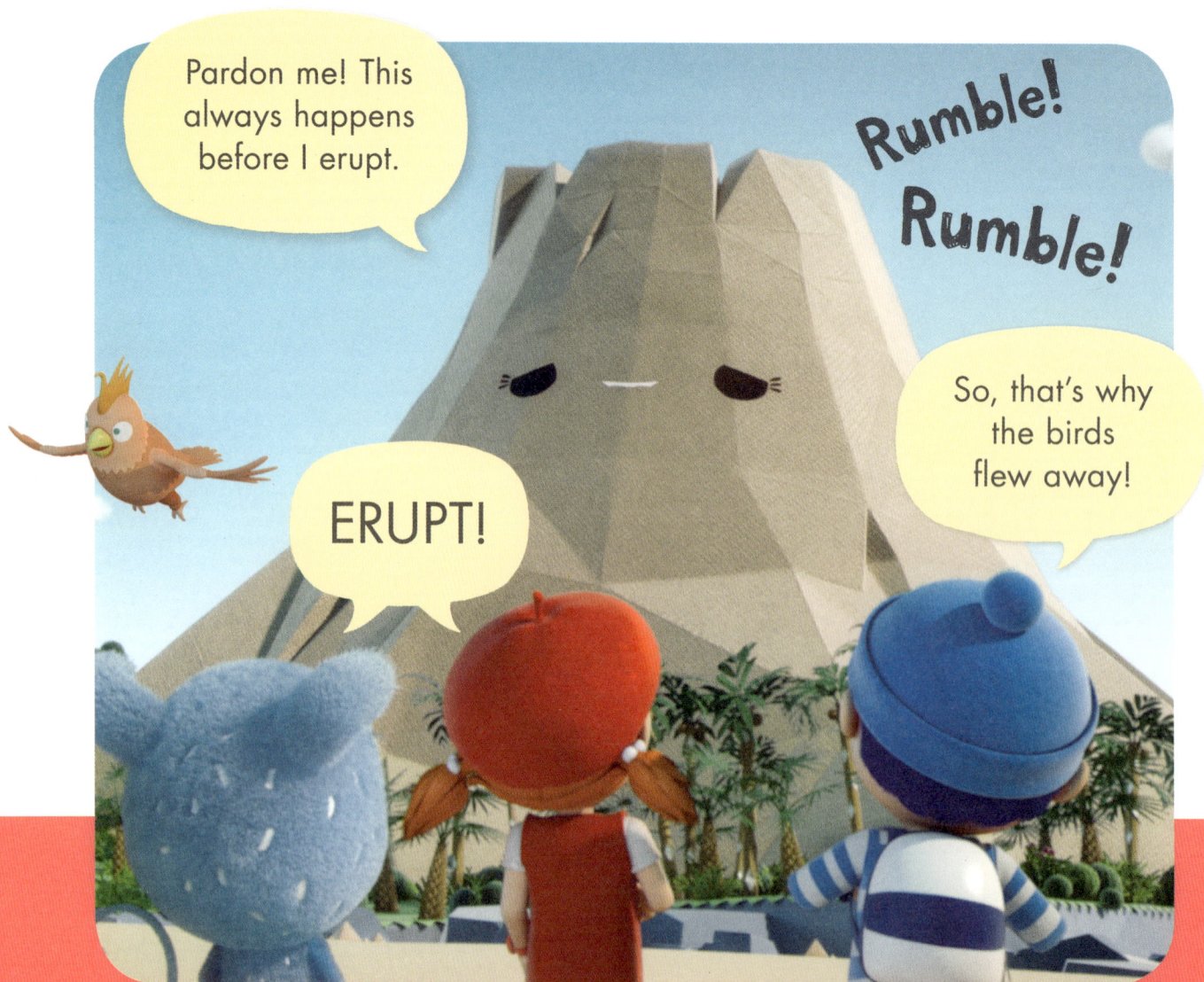

Messy thought an eruption sounded fun, but Zoe thought it sounded dangerous! She called Zim on her communicator.

Zim, we're beside a volcano that's about to erupt!

DON'T PANIC! We're on our way!

Before long, they spotted the cloudship *speeding* towards the island.

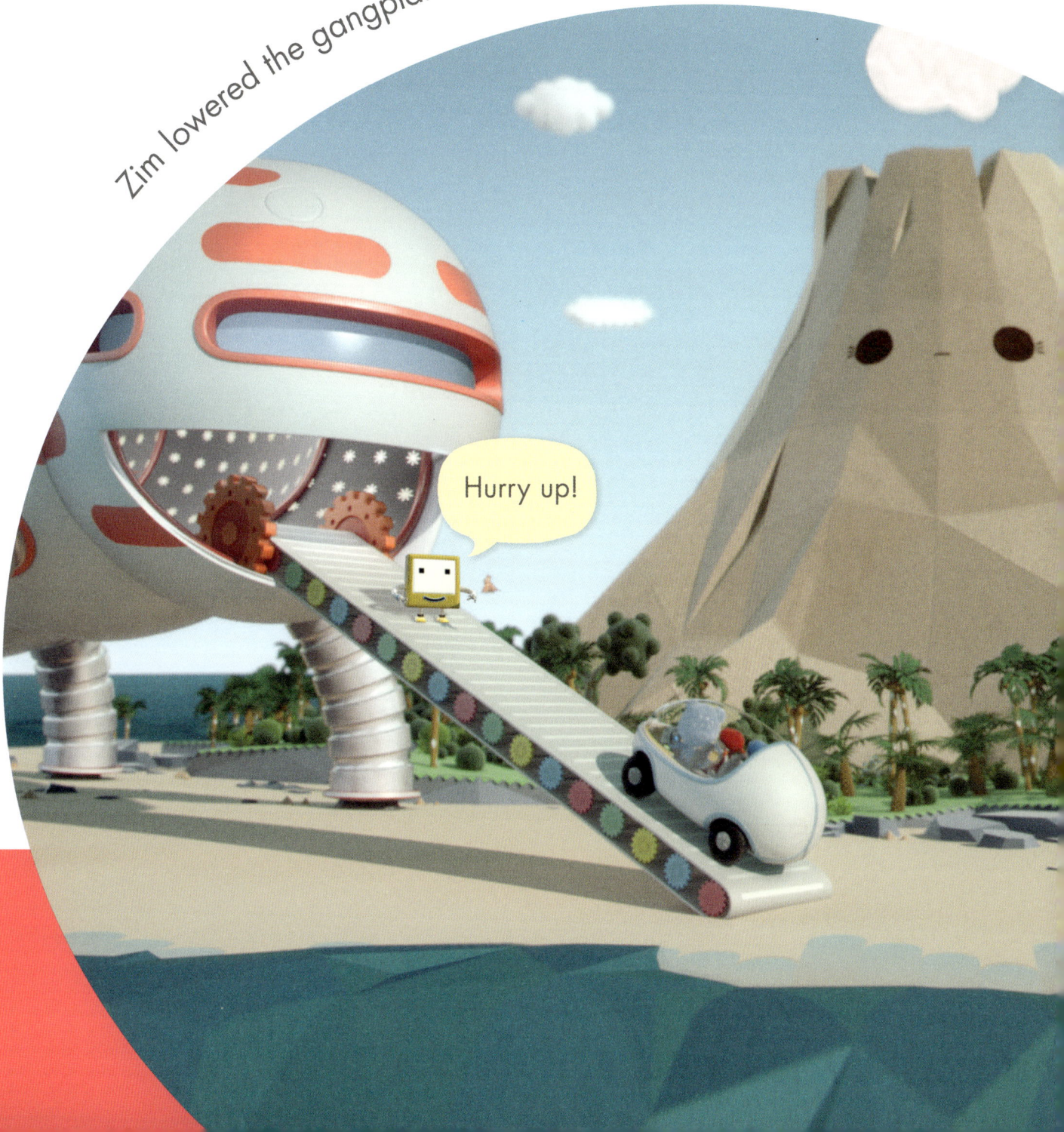

Zim lowered the gangplank and Okidoodle **zoomed** inside.

Suddenly, there was a deep **rumbling** sound and
the ground shuddered and **shook** more than ever.
The gang rushed to their seats ready for take off.

Tweet! Tweet!

Hold tight.
It's going
to get bumpy!

As they lifted into the air, the little bird started **fluttering** and tweeting in front of the window. She was trying to tell them something again.

What's wrong, little bird?

Oh no! A group of animals was stranded on the beach!
They needed to be rescued before Vivian erupted.

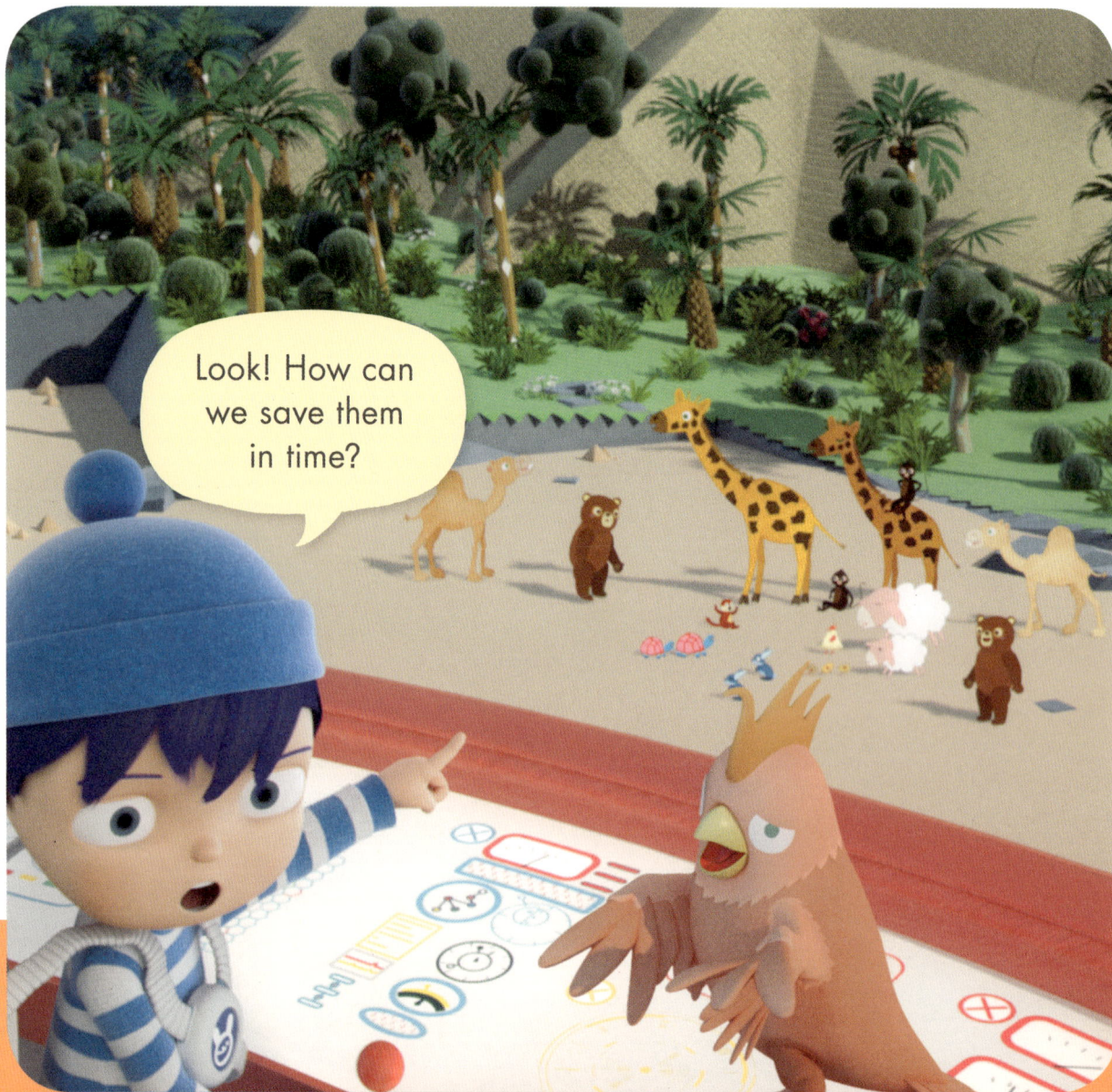

I think I have an idea ...

Zam disappeared into her workshop. After a lot of banging and sawing she revealed a **giant** plug.

Ugh! I feel all bunged up!

Carefully, they lowered the plug into the hole in Vivian's top. It held back the eruption ... but not for long!

They had to save the animals before Vivian erupted!
Zim herded them up the gangplank into the cloudship.

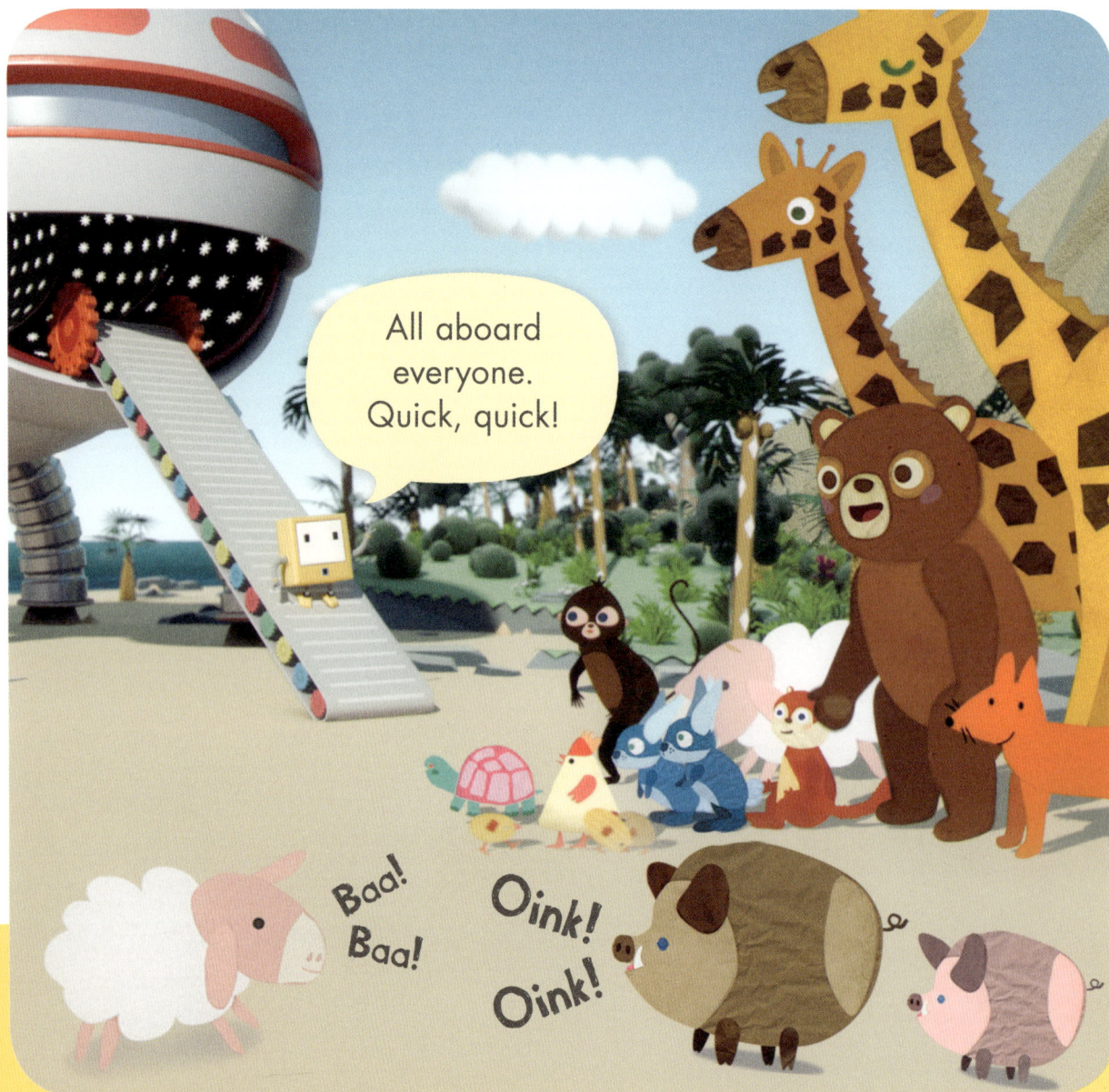

When all the animals were safely inside, Messy gave Zam the signal to remove the **giant** plug.

Okay, Zam. Let her blow!

The plug came out with a **POP**! There was a shudder and a **BOOM**! Red-hot rock shot out of Vivian's top. The cloudship had to swerve out of the way.

Pop!

Boom!

After a while the shuddering stopped. The eruption was over and Vivian heaved a sigh of relief.

The animals were soon safely back on the beach.
Then the little bird spotted her flock. The clever birds
were returning to the island now it was safe.

Tweet!

Thanks for your
help, little bird!

Zam asked Vivian to tell the little bird if she ever felt **rumbly** again. With the bird's help the gang could race to the rescue with their **giant** plug!

Goodbye animals!

Goodbye Vivian! It has been quite an adventure!

The end

What is a volcano?

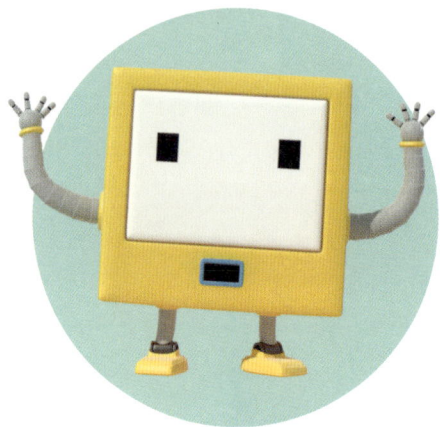

A volcano is a mountain with red-hot rock inside it. The rock is so hot it has turned to liquid. It is called **lava**.

What is an eruption?

An **eruption** is when lava explodes out of the top of a volcano.

Why do volcanoes erupt?

Sometimes, pressure builds up under a volcano, making bubbles of gas. The bubbles explode out of the top, taking **lava** with them.

Zam's workshop

A bottle of fizzy drink can erupt like a volcano. Try this!

Do this outside!

Shake the bottle to mix up the bubbles of gas in the drink.

Open the lid and the bubbles and drink erupt out of the top.

Giggle with the gang!

What happens when you tell a volcano a joke?

It will lava lot!

What did the mummy volcano say to the little volcano?

It's rude to erupt when I'm talking!

First published in the United Kingdom in 2016 by Thames & Hudson Ltd, 181A High Holborn, London WC1V 7QX

Licensed by Doodle Productions Limited based on the TV series 'Messy Goes to OKIDO'

Volcanic panic © 2016 Thames & Hudson Ltd, London

OKIDO content and logo © 2016 Doodle Productions Limited

OKIDO and MESSY GOES TO OKIDO are trademarks of Doodle Productions Limited

Printed and bound in China by C&C Offset Printing Co. Ltd

British Library Cataloguing-in-Publication Data
A catalogue record for this book is available from the British Library

ISBN 978-0-500-65084-4

To find out about all our publications, please visit www.thamesandhudson.com. There you can subscribe to our e-newsletter, browse or download our current catalogue, and buy any titles that are in print.